This is the story of a remarkable baseball team from Springfield, Massachusetts, and its star player—a boy named Bunny who was the only African-American on the team.

The year was 1934, a time very different from today. Throughout much of the United States, and especially in the South, white children and black children went to separate schools. Many businesses, including hotels and restaurants, refused to serve black people. They even had to drink from different water fountains.

In those days, no major league baseball teams had black players. It was not until 1947 that a talented second baseman named Jackie Robinson was signed by the Brooklyn Dodgers. Jackie became the first African-American to play in the modern major leagues.

People were fighting for equal rights off the field as well. In 1955, a courageous black woman named Rosa Parks was arrested for refusing to move to the back of a bus. The seats in the front were reserved for white people.

On August 28, 1963, more than three hundred thousand people marched with Dr. Martin Luther King, Jr. to the Lincoln Memorial in Washington D.C. On that hot summer afternoon, Dr. King delivered his historic "I Have a Dream" speech, calling for a day when people would be judged "not by the color of their skin, but by the content of their character."

Although the story of Bunny Taliaferro and his remarkable Springfield team is not widely known, it honors and celebrates an important event in the history of America's struggle for racial equality.

Dedications

To Diane, the heart and soul of our team.
Richard Andersen

To my dear mother, Elnora Purnell.
As a church officer, Girl Scout leader, choir leader, wife, mother, grandmother, and
great-grandmother, she has always given of herself in serving others.
Her loving nature and beautiful smile touch everyone she meets.
I love you, Mom.
Gerald Purnell

In memory of Judge Daniel "Danny" Keyes (1909-2012)
Team Member, American Legion Post 21, Summer of 1934
"It wasn't just the right thing to do. It was the only thing to do. If we'd gone ahead without
Bunny, even if we had won the championship, no one would ever have heard of us."

A Home Run For
Bunny

Story by Richard Andersen

Illustrated by Gerald Purnell

I never liked Bunny Taliaferro. How could you with a name like Bunny? He wasn't even Italian! His real name was Ernest, but everyone called him Bunny because all he did was run.

Everywhere! To and from school, on errands for his mom and dad. He even ran around the block while waiting for his friends to come out and play.

Yes, Bunny could run. Fast! And he could throw, too. When we were only eight, I saw him hurl a snowball from across his backyard to keep a squirrel from stealing the birdseed.

Bunny's first baseball mitt was the old-fashioned kind with three fingers. His mom had to stuff it with rags and lace it back up before he could use it. An old tire his dad hung from a tree in their backyard became Bunny's first strike zone.

But baseball was Bunny's specialty. Throwing strikes came as easy to him as hurling hardballs through that old tire in his backyard. As a freshman, he went undefeated and pitched a complete game every time he took the mound.

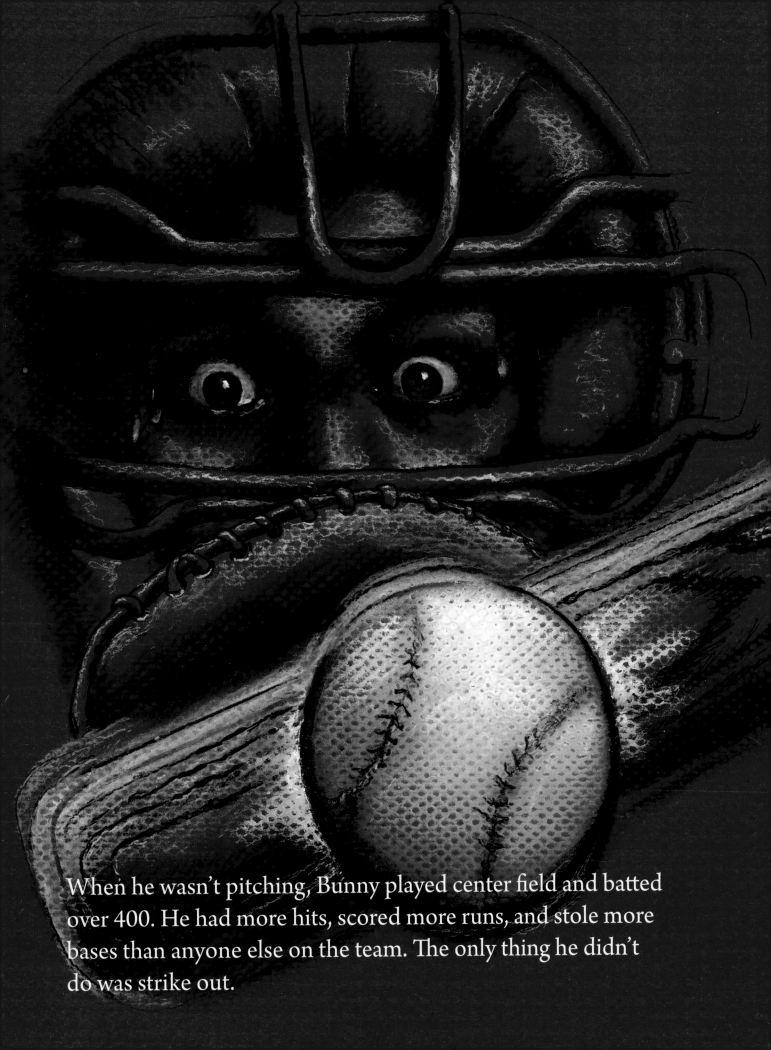

When he wasn't pitching, Bunny played center field and batted over 400. He had more hits, scored more runs, and stole more bases than anyone else on the team. The only thing he didn't do was strike out.

Baseball was my specialty too, and though my team wasn't as good as Bunny's, we won every game I pitched. When the school season ended, we were both picked for the American Legion All-Star team. Who would've guessed we'd wind up wearing the same colors after competing against each other so many times!

Both of us pitched really well all summer, but I had to warm the bench between my starts while Bunny made a name for himself playing center field. With his amazing speed, he was able to catch balls other outfielders could never have reached. He also threw out a lot of base runners who normally would have been safe. I hated to admit it, but Bunny really was the better athlete.

Our team lost only once
all summer, and it was one
of the games I pitched.
Wouldn't you know it!

After taking the league title, we sailed through the Massachusetts
Championship Series with Bunny tossing shutouts in both games.

Bunny pitched another shutout in the opening game of the New
England Championship Series. Along with stroking two home runs
and stealing six bases, he even picked off a runner at third. How
often have you seen a pitcher do that?

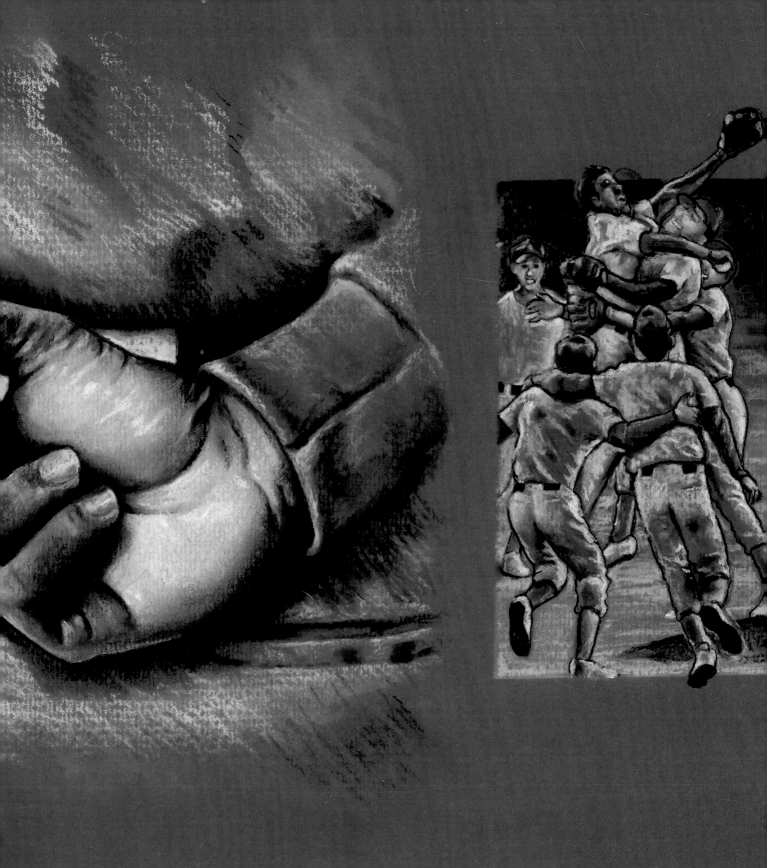

The next day I did something Bunny never did: allow only four hits and one walk in an eleven-inning shutout. Next stop: the Eastern Regionals in Gastonia, North Carolina.

When we boarded the train with Coach Steere and our team manager, Mr. Harris, we were all a little nervous, but also very excited. None of us had ever traveled so far from home before. All I knew about North Carolina was that it was south of Massachusetts.

We knew something was wrong just after the train pulled into Gastonia. The band that had been playing walked off as soon as they saw Bunny step onto the platform. Then the bus pulled away, leaving us stranded. We had to carry our bags and equipment all the way to the hotel.

When we got to the hotel, the manager told Mr. Harris, "Colored folks ain't allowed to sleep here, so we've arranged for your boy to stay with the local Negro doctor."

"Bunny is a member of this team," Mr. Harris replied. "Where the team goes, he goes."

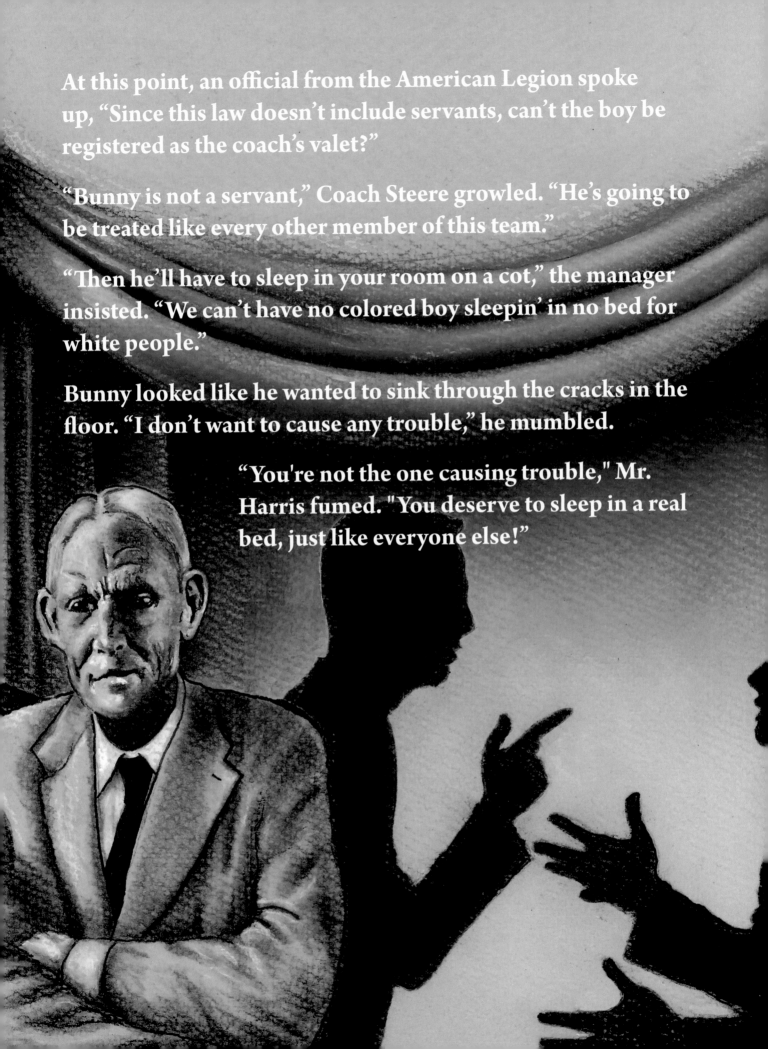

At this point, an official from the American Legion spoke up, "Since this law doesn't include servants, can't the boy be registered as the coach's valet?"

"Bunny is not a servant," Coach Steere growled. "He's going to be treated like every other member of this team."

"Then he'll have to sleep in your room on a cot," the manager insisted. "We can't have no colored boy sleepin' in no bed for white people."

Bunny looked like he wanted to sink through the cracks in the floor. "I don't want to cause any trouble," he mumbled.

"You're not the one causing trouble," Mr. Harris fumed. "You deserve to sleep in a real bed, just like everyone else!"

That afternoon we held our first practice. More than 2,000 people showed up to watch. That was a bigger crowd than we'd had at all our games back home put together. And were they mad! Steaming!

"You boys done played your last game!" one man shouted. Others threatened to tear the shirts off our backs if Bunny even stepped onto the field. One usher told me that the Ku Klux Klan was planning to kidnap us from the hotel, and our families would never hear from us again.

Some of the boys were really scared. I was too. Baseball wasn't worth getting killed over. At the same time, something deep inside me wanted to prove that we could beat any team in the tournament.

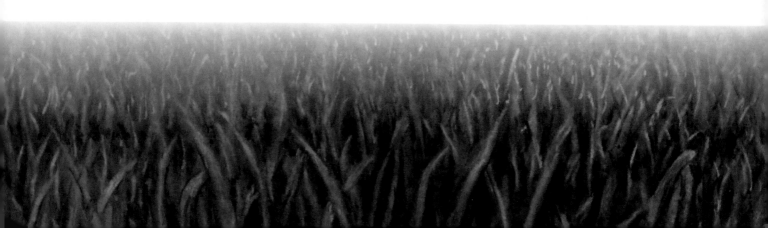

Bunny was the first to make a move. He grabbed his bat, stepped up to the plate, and started taking cuts at imaginary pitches. When Coach Steere told us to take our positions on the field, for once I was glad to be warming the bench.

More threats and jeers filled the air as Coach made his way to the mound: "Batter up!" he called. Bunny lined the first pitch over the left-field fence. That silenced the crowd, but only for a second. Coach Steere threw his second pitch, and Bunny airmailed that one out of the park too. Special delivery to the people of Gastonia!

The more noise the crowd made, the smoother Bunny swung. He hit six home runs on six pitches. That's when it started raining soda bottles, tin cans, and half-eaten hotdogs.

More trouble greeted us when we got back to the hotel. The teams from Maryland and Florida announced that they wouldn't play against us if Bunny was allowed on the field. We also found out that we couldn't go to the Welcome Banquet if Bunny was with the team.

To make matters worse, the American Legion official didn't think the police would be able to protect us from the crowds.

"Your boy is the only Negro player in the tournament," he told Mr. Harris. "What if he hits a batter with a pitch? What if he slides into somebody trying to steal a base?"

"What if Bunny pitches a no-hitter?" Mr. Harris snapped back. "What if he scores the winning run?"

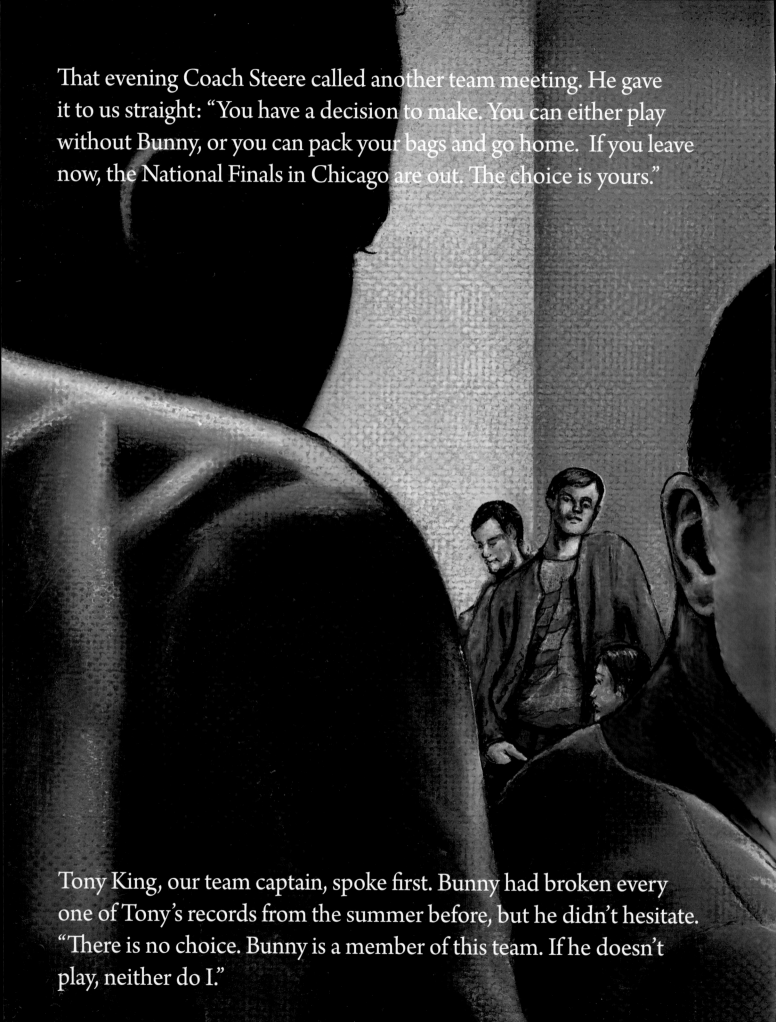

That evening Coach Steere called another team meeting. He gave it to us straight: "You have a decision to make. You can either play without Bunny, or you can pack your bags and go home. If you leave now, the National Finals in Chicago are out. The choice is yours."

Tony King, our team captain, spoke first. Bunny had broken every one of Tony's records from the summer before, but he didn't hesitate. "There is no choice. Bunny is a member of this team. If he doesn't play, neither do I."

I knew I could have pitched us to victory in Gastonia, but I also voted to go home. So did every other player. Bunny came through for us all summer long, and now it was our turn to do the same for him.

That night, we snuck out of the hotel and caught a train heading north. It had to make a special stop just for us.

Bunny was the first to speak: "I know you guys wanted that championship as bad as I did. But having teammates like you is more important than winning any ball game. You guys aren't just teammates, you're friends—the best friends anyone could ever have."

News of what had happened in North Carolina reached Springfield before we did. When the train pulled into Union Station, a huge crowd—even bigger than the one in Gastonia—was waiting to greet us. The people cheered wildly and held up signs calling us HEROES and CHAMPS. Flashbulbs lit up the night like fireworks.

Looking back now, nothing we did on any ball field compares with what we did on August 23, 1934. Long before anyone had ever heard of Jackie Robinson, a team of fifteen-year-old kids from Springfield, Massachusetts, chose loyalty and respect over championships. Without swinging a single bat, we'd hit a home run—not just for Bunny, but for people everywhere.

ISBN 978-0-9855417-2-9

PUBLISHING COMPANY, L.L.C.

P.O Box 1865 ● Bellevue, WA 98009

Tel: 425-968-5097 ● Fax: 425-968-5634

liteinfo@illumin.com ● www.illumin.com

Publisher's Appreciation

A heartfelt thanks to our outstanding editing team – Kelley Frodel, Siri Alderson, Londa Ogden, Stuart Moore, Megan Hyde, Ian Wyant, Julie Ropelewski, Jacklyn Grambush, Cristina Ralston, Ashley Goodwin, Dr. Gloria Burgess, and Diane Lyn Andersen. The final stages of creating this beautiful book were greatly enhanced by the creative and dedicated services provided by Haley Larson, Breanna Powell, and Mie Morikubo.

Thanks also to Coach Brian Collins, whose support and input has been invaluable, Conner Cormier who was the model for Bunny, and to Tony King and Danny Keyes for their impeccable memories of the actual events that transpired in 1934.

John and Kimmie Thompson

Special Acknowledgement

This beautiful book has been brought to life through the energy, editing expertise, and financial support of our editorial director, Ruth E. Thompson. "When I first read the poignant story submitted by Richard Andersen, I knew it could be a truly important book that would inspire adults as well as children. I would like to dedicate this book to the memory of my husband, Charles Arthur (Art) Thompson. In addition to being a wonderful husband, he was a dedicated father, grandfather, and school administrator—as well as being an avid sportsman."

First Printing 2013
Published in the United States of America
Printed in China by Chenxi International Industrial, Ltd.
Book Designer: Mie Morikubo

More inspiring picture books from Illumination Arts

Am I a Color Too?
Heidi Cole/Nancy Vogl/Gerald Purnell
ISBN 978-0-9740190-5-5
A young interracial boy wonders why people are labeled by the color of their skin. Seeing that people dream, feel, sing, dance, and love regardless of their color, he asks, *Am I a Color, Too?*

God's Promise
Maureen Moss/Gerald Purnell
ISBN 978-0-9740190-7-9
Before her birth, God helps Angelina prepare for her wondrous new life on Earth.

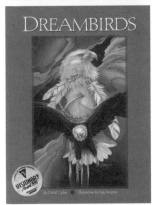

Dreambirds
David Ogden/Jody Bergsma
ISBN 978-0-935699-09-8
Young Natsama must overcome many challenges and obstacles before he finally finds his elusive dreambird and can claim his mysterious gift. This masterfully illustrated Native American story captivates readers of all ages.

One Voice
Cindy McKinley/Mary Gregg Byrne
ISBN 978-0-9855417-0-5
A young boy's dedication to peace and kindness ignites a chain reaction of generosity that uplifts his entire community.

INSPIRE EVERY CHILD FOUNDATION
A portion of the profits from this book will be donated to Inspire Every Child, a non-profit foundation dedicated to helping disadvantaged children around the world. This organization provides non-denominational, inspirational books to organizations that are directly involved in supporting the welfare of children. Your help in supporting this worthwhile cause is greatly appreciated. Please visit www.inspire-every-child.org.

In each of his four years at Springfield Technical High School, Ernest "Bunny" Taliaferro lettered in football, basketball, and baseball. Bunny was named All-City in football, and his team won championships in 1934 and 1935. In baseball, he was undefeated as a pitcher and led his team in hitting and home runs each year.

Although offered several college scholarships, Bunny stayed in Springfield, where he played Triple-A baseball for a number of years. He married his high school sweetheart, and together they raised six children, five of whom graduated from college. Bunny died on November 19, 1967—his fiftieth birthday.

Bunny Taliaferro was not just a great athlete; he was a remarkable human being who inspired everyone around him. Today a monument honoring Bunny, his teammates, and their historic response to racism stands beside the baseball field in Springfield's Forest Park.

In 2010, the Springfield Post 21 American Legion team was revived after having been disbanded in 1935 to protest the national organization's tolerance of racial discrimination. At the opening day game on June 13th, Tony King and Danny Keyes, the two surviving members of the 1934 team, threw the ceremonial first pitches.

Before the game, Governor Deval Patrick awarded championship rings to Tony, Danny, and Bunny's daughter, Linda Taliaferro. "What those kids said so loudly in 1934 resonates through the decades," Ms. Taliaferro told the crowd. "And in one voice."

On August 22, 2010, Tony and Danny were again asked to throw ceremonial first pitches, this time at a Boston Red Sox game in Fenway Park—a notable change from earlier days when Boston was the only major league team without an African-American player.

Cover Image: The players shown in the background are the actual boys who represented Springfield Post 21 in the American Legion Championships of 1934. From left to right they are: Jimmy Lawler, Franny Luce, Bobby Triggs, Captain Tony King, Danny Keyes, Kaiser Lombardi, Johnny Coffey, Ray O'Shay, Joe Kelly, Franny O'Connell, John Malaguiti, Louis Grondolski, Freddy Laczek, and Joe Kogut. Mascot Joe Carmody is seated in front.